AF824772

TO CULTIVATE SUCCESS

IN ALL AREAS OF LIFE

THROUGH CONSTANT LEARNING

SO THAT PEOPLE MAY LIVE LIFE

HAPPIER AND HEALTHIER.

TheTradersWire.com
PO Box 2854
Denver, CO 80209

email: info@thetraderswire.com
www.thetraderswire.com

A SPECIAL THANK YOU TO ALL THE DEDICATED TRADERS

WHO MAKE THIS BUSINESS BOTH THE MOST CHALLENGING

AND MOST REWARDING.

"What beat me was not having brains enough to stick to my own game - that is, to play the market only when I was satisfied that precedents favored my play.... There is the plain fool, who does the wrong thing at all times everywhere, but there is also the Wall Street fool, who thinks he must trade all the time. No man can have adequate reasons for buying or selling stocks daily - or sufficient knowledge to make his play an intelligent play."

– Jesse Livermore, Reminiscences of a Stock Operator by Edwin Lefèvre

WHY A TRADER'S JOURNAL?

The truth is, trading is one of the very few pursuits in life that is truly zero-sum. For you to win, someone has to lose. It can also provide the greatest financial rewards of any business on the planet. This one-two punch of always having a winner and a loser combined with unlimited wealth creates the most competitive business anywhere. The only way to succeed in trading is by constant learning. Every trade you make, both winners and losers, holds the key to your success.

Each trade you make is full of hidden gems of knowledge and insight. The question is, how do you gain access to those hidden gems? It is not by simply writing each trade down as this does not provide anything concrete from which to learn. The answer is by journaling. Only when you document each trade, the results and your thoughts, can you begin to see the gems through the muck. A journal will document your wins, losses, struggles, market setups, conditions, and all the elements that will eventually guide you to success.

THE JOURNAL DESIGNED FOR SUCCESS

This trading journal was specifically designed to track your trading activity and help you uncover those hidden gems. It gives you the opportunity to double your trading efforts. Once, the actual trades, and again through your written history. The trade journal pages were designed to be flexible enough for stock, option, futures, and even forex trading. You should complete a trade journal page for each trade you place. The Trader's Journal gives you not only the trade setup specifics, but your own thoughts and analysis can be included for each trade. It also includes a notes section to journal your thoughts and emotions around each trade. This journal will help you clarify your thoughts and assess whether you are working towards your goals or not.

THE JOURNAL FOR CLARITY

Consider that success in trading typically requires purely analytical skills; emotions often get in the way. When you journal, it allows you to really separate the analytics of a trade from the emotions of the trade. If you have losing trades, which you will, journaling will help you separate the emotions of losing money from the trade. It will allow you to get the details out of your brain and down on paper. That cleared space will allow your brain to process the trade better and discover the corrections needed to prevent the loss again in the future. By clearing your mind, it will also allow you to better analyze future trades without the clouded judgement of past failed trades. The Trader's Journal empties the mind and allows your precious resources to problem solve rather than problem store.

The Trader's Wire is your source for daily news and support in your success with trading. If you are not getting The Wire, TheTradersWire.com's daily news service, then you are missing the most important news affecting the market and your money.

We are here to support you and your trading through better education and information.

TheTradersWire.com

DATE	GOALS

TRADEJOURNAL

/ / MTWTFSS

TRADE RESULT

PROFIT / LOSS: $

MARKET SENTIMENT

TRADE PLAN

LONG SHORT SPREAD

SYMBOL:

ENTRY PRICE:

TARGET PRICE:

STOP LOSS:

CLOSE PRICE:

STRATEGY:

SETUP CHART

ENTRY TIME: : AM/PM

CLOSE TIME: : AM/PM

PURCHASE PRICE:

CLOSING PRICE:

COMMISSION:

TRADE ANALYSIS

PERSONAL NOTES

/ / MTWTFSS

MARKET SENTIMENT 

TRADE PLAN

LONG SHORT SPREAD

SYMBOL:

ENTRY PRICE:

TARGET PRICE:

STOP LOSS:

CLOSE PRICE:

STRATEGY:

SETUP CHART

ENTRY TIME: : AM/PM

CLOSE TIME: : AM/PM

PURCHASE PRICE:

CLOSING PRICE:

COMMISSION:

TRADE RESULT

PROFIT / LOSS: $

TRADE ANALYSIS

PERSONAL NOTES

TRADEJOURNAL

/ / **M T W T F S S**

MARKET SENTIMENT

TRADE PLAN

LONG SHORT SPREAD

SYMBOL:

ENTRY PRICE:

TARGET PRICE:

STOP LOSS:

CLOSE PRICE:

STRATEGY:

SETUP CHART

ENTRY TIME: : AM/PM

CLOSE TIME: : AM/PM

PURCHASE PRICE:

CLOSING PRICE:

COMMISSION:

TRADE RESULT

PROFIT / LOSS: $

TRADE ANALYSIS

PERSONAL NOTES

/ / M T W T F S S

MARKET SENTIMENT

TRADE PLAN

LONG SHORT SPREAD

SYMBOL:

ENTRY PRICE:

TARGET PRICE:

STOP LOSS:

CLOSE PRICE:

STRATEGY:

SETUP CHART

ENTRY TIME: : AM/PM

CLOSE TIME: : AM/PM

PURCHASE PRICE:

CLOSING PRICE:

COMMISSION:

TRADE RESULT

PROFIT / LOSS: $

TRADE ANALYSIS

PERSONAL NOTES

TRADEJOURNAL

/ / **M T W T F S S**

MARKET SENTIMENT

TRADE PLAN

LONG SHORT SPREAD

SYMBOL:

ENTRY PRICE:

TARGET PRICE:

STOP LOSS:

CLOSE PRICE:

STRATEGY:

SETUP CHART

ENTRY TIME: : AM/PM

CLOSE TIME: : AM/PM

PURCHASE PRICE:

CLOSING PRICE:

COMMISSION:

TRADE RESULT

PROFIT / LOSS: $

TRADE ANALYSIS

PERSONAL NOTES

/ / MTWTFSS

MARKET SENTIMENT 

TRADE PLAN

LONG SHORT SPREAD

SYMBOL:

ENTRY PRICE:

TARGET PRICE:

STOP LOSS:

CLOSE PRICE:

STRATEGY:

SETUP CHART

ENTRY TIME: : AM/PM

CLOSE TIME: : AM/PM

PURCHASE PRICE:

CLOSING PRICE:

COMMISSION:

TRADE RESULT

PROFIT / LOSS: $

TRADE ANALYSIS

PERSONAL NOTES

TRADEJOURNAL

/ / **M T W T F S S**

MARKET SENTIMENT 

TRADE PLAN

LONG SHORT SPREAD

SYMBOL:

ENTRY PRICE:

TARGET PRICE:

STOP LOSS:

CLOSE PRICE:

STRATEGY:

SETUP CHART

ENTRY TIME: : AM/PM

CLOSE TIME: : AM/PM

PURCHASE PRICE:

CLOSING PRICE:

COMMISSION:

TRADE RESULT

PROFIT / LOSS: $

TRADE ANALYSIS

PERSONAL NOTES

/ / M T W T F S S

MARKET SENTIMENT 

TRADE PLAN

LONG SHORT SPREAD

SYMBOL:

ENTRY PRICE:

TARGET PRICE:

STOP LOSS:

CLOSE PRICE:

STRATEGY:

SETUP CHART

ENTRY TIME: : AM/PM

CLOSE TIME: : AM/PM

PURCHASE PRICE:

CLOSING PRICE:

COMMISSION:

TRADE RESULT

PROFIT / LOSS: $

TRADE ANALYSIS

PERSONAL NOTES

TRADEJOURNAL

/ / **M T W T F S S**

MARKET SENTIMENT

TRADE PLAN

LONG SHORT SPREAD

SYMBOL:

ENTRY PRICE:

TARGET PRICE:

STOP LOSS:

CLOSE PRICE:

STRATEGY:

SETUP CHART

ENTRY TIME: : AM/PM

CLOSE TIME: : AM/PM

PURCHASE PRICE:

CLOSING PRICE:

COMMISSION:

TRADE RESULT

PROFIT / LOSS: $

TRADE ANALYSIS

PERSONAL NOTES

/ / MTWTFSS

MARKET SENTIMENT

TRADE PLAN

LONG SHORT SPREAD

SYMBOL:

ENTRY PRICE:

TARGET PRICE:

STOP LOSS:

CLOSE PRICE:

STRATEGY:

SETUP CHART

ENTRY TIME: : AM/PM

CLOSE TIME: : AM/PM

PURCHASE PRICE:

CLOSING PRICE:

COMMISSION:

TRADE RESULT

PROFIT / LOSS: $

TRADE ANALYSIS

PERSONAL NOTES

TRADEJOURNAL

/ / **M T W T F S S**

MARKET SENTIMENT

TRADE PLAN

LONG SHORT SPREAD

SYMBOL:

ENTRY PRICE:

TARGET PRICE:

STOP LOSS:

CLOSE PRICE:

STRATEGY:

SETUP CHART

ENTRY TIME: : AM/PM

CLOSE TIME: : AM/PM

PURCHASE PRICE:

CLOSING PRICE:

COMMISSION:

TRADE RESULT

PROFIT / LOSS: $

TRADE ANALYSIS

PERSONAL NOTES

/ / M T W T F S S

MARKET SENTIMENT 

TRADE PLAN

LONG SHORT SPREAD

SYMBOL:

ENTRY PRICE:

TARGET PRICE:

STOP LOSS:

CLOSE PRICE:

STRATEGY:

SETUP CHART

ENTRY TIME: : AM/PM

CLOSE TIME: : AM/PM

PURCHASE PRICE:

CLOSING PRICE:

COMMISSION:

TRADE RESULT

PROFIT / LOSS: $

TRADE ANALYSIS

PERSONAL NOTES

TRADEJOURNAL

/ / M T W T F S S

MARKET SENTIMENT 

TRADE PLAN

LONG SHORT SPREAD

SYMBOL:

ENTRY PRICE:

TARGET PRICE:

STOP LOSS:

CLOSE PRICE:

STRATEGY:

SETUP CHART

ENTRY TIME: : AM/PM

CLOSE TIME: : AM/PM

PURCHASE PRICE:

CLOSING PRICE:

COMMISSION:

TRADE RESULT

PROFIT / LOSS: $

TRADE ANALYSIS

PERSONAL NOTES

/ / M T W T F S S

MARKET SENTIMENT

TRADE PLAN

LONG SHORT SPREAD

SYMBOL:

ENTRY PRICE:

TARGET PRICE:

STOP LOSS:

CLOSE PRICE:

STRATEGY:

SETUP CHART

ENTRY TIME: : AM/PM

CLOSE TIME: : AM/PM

PURCHASE PRICE:

CLOSING PRICE:

COMMISSION:

TRADE RESULT

PROFIT / LOSS: $

TRADE ANALYSIS

PERSONAL NOTES

TRADEJOURNAL

/ / **M T W T F S S**

MARKET SENTIMENT 

TRADE PLAN

LONG SHORT SPREAD

SYMBOL:

ENTRY PRICE:

TARGET PRICE:

STOP LOSS:

CLOSE PRICE:

STRATEGY:

SETUP CHART

ENTRY TIME: : AM/PM

CLOSE TIME: : AM/PM

PURCHASE PRICE:

CLOSING PRICE:

COMMISSION:

TRADE RESULT

PROFIT / LOSS: $

TRADE ANALYSIS

PERSONAL NOTES

/ / MTWTFSS

MARKET SENTIMENT

TRADE PLAN

LONG SHORT SPREAD

SYMBOL:

ENTRY PRICE:

TARGET PRICE:

STOP LOSS:

CLOSE PRICE:

STRATEGY:

SETUP CHART

ENTRY TIME: : AM/PM

CLOSE TIME: : AM/PM

PURCHASE PRICE:

CLOSING PRICE:

COMMISSION:

TRADE RESULT

PROFIT / LOSS: $

TRADE ANALYSIS

PERSONAL NOTES

TRADEJOURNAL

/ / **M T W T F S S**

MARKET SENTIMENT

TRADE PLAN

LONG SHORT SPREAD

SYMBOL:

ENTRY PRICE:

TARGET PRICE:

STOP LOSS:

CLOSE PRICE:

STRATEGY:

SETUP CHART

ENTRY TIME: : AM/PM

CLOSE TIME: : AM/PM

PURCHASE PRICE:

CLOSING PRICE:

COMMISSION:

TRADE RESULT

PROFIT / LOSS: $

TRADE ANALYSIS

PERSONAL NOTES

/ / M T W T F S S

MARKET SENTIMENT 

TRADE PLAN

LONG SHORT SPREAD

SYMBOL:

ENTRY PRICE:

TARGET PRICE:

STOP LOSS:

CLOSE PRICE:

STRATEGY:

SETUP CHART

ENTRY TIME: : AM/PM

CLOSE TIME: : AM/PM

PURCHASE PRICE:

CLOSING PRICE:

COMMISSION:

TRADE RESULT

PROFIT / LOSS: $

TRADE ANALYSIS

PERSONAL NOTES

TRADEJOURNAL

/ / **M T W T F S S**

MARKET SENTIMENT

TRADE PLAN

LONG SHORT SPREAD

SYMBOL:

ENTRY PRICE:

TARGET PRICE:

STOP LOSS:

CLOSE PRICE:

STRATEGY:

SETUP CHART

ENTRY TIME: : AM/PM

CLOSE TIME: : AM/PM

PURCHASE PRICE:

CLOSING PRICE:

COMMISSION:

TRADE RESULT

PROFIT / LOSS: $

TRADE ANALYSIS

PERSONAL NOTES

/ / M T W T F S S

MARKET SENTIMENT 

TRADE PLAN

LONG SHORT SPREAD

SYMBOL:

ENTRY PRICE:

TARGET PRICE:

STOP LOSS:

CLOSE PRICE:

STRATEGY:

SETUP CHART

ENTRY TIME: : AM/PM

CLOSE TIME: : AM/PM

PURCHASE PRICE:

CLOSING PRICE:

COMMISSION:

TRADE RESULT

PROFIT / LOSS: $

TRADE ANALYSIS

PERSONAL NOTES

TRADEJOURNAL

/ / **M T W T F S S**

MARKET SENTIMENT 

TRADE PLAN

LONG SHORT SPREAD

SYMBOL:

ENTRY PRICE:

TARGET PRICE:

STOP LOSS:

CLOSE PRICE:

STRATEGY:

SETUP CHART

ENTRY TIME: : AM/PM

CLOSE TIME: : AM/PM

PURCHASE PRICE:

CLOSING PRICE:

COMMISSION:

TRADE RESULT

PROFIT / LOSS: $

TRADE ANALYSIS

PERSONAL NOTES

/ / M T W T F S S

MARKET SENTIMENT 

TRADE PLAN

LONG SHORT SPREAD

SYMBOL:

ENTRY PRICE:

TARGET PRICE:

STOP LOSS:

CLOSE PRICE:

STRATEGY:

SETUP CHART

ENTRY TIME: : AM/PM

CLOSE TIME: : AM/PM

PURCHASE PRICE:

CLOSING PRICE:

COMMISSION:

TRADE RESULT

PROFIT / LOSS: $

TRADE ANALYSIS

PERSONAL NOTES

TRADEJOURNAL

/ / **M T W T F S S**

MARKET SENTIMENT 

TRADE PLAN

LONG SHORT SPREAD

SYMBOL:

ENTRY PRICE:

TARGET PRICE:

STOP LOSS:

CLOSE PRICE:

STRATEGY:

SETUP CHART

ENTRY TIME: : AM/PM

CLOSE TIME: : AM/PM

PURCHASE PRICE:

CLOSING PRICE:

COMMISSION:

TRADE RESULT

PROFIT / LOSS: $

TRADE ANALYSIS

PERSONAL NOTES

/ / M T W T F S S

MARKET SENTIMENT 

TRADE PLAN

LONG SHORT SPREAD

SYMBOL:

ENTRY PRICE:

TARGET PRICE:

STOP LOSS:

CLOSE PRICE:

STRATEGY:

SETUP CHART

ENTRY TIME: : AM/PM

CLOSE TIME: : AM/PM

PURCHASE PRICE:

CLOSING PRICE:

COMMISSION:

TRADE RESULT

PROFIT / LOSS: $

TRADE ANALYSIS

PERSONAL NOTES

TRADEJOURNAL

/ / **M T W T F S S**

MARKET SENTIMENT 

TRADE PLAN

LONG SHORT SPREAD

SYMBOL:

ENTRY PRICE:

TARGET PRICE:

STOP LOSS:

CLOSE PRICE:

STRATEGY:

SETUP CHART

ENTRY TIME: : AM/PM

CLOSE TIME: : AM/PM

PURCHASE PRICE:

CLOSING PRICE:

COMMISSION:

TRADE RESULT

PROFIT / LOSS: $

TRADE ANALYSIS

PERSONAL NOTES

/ / MTWTFSS

MARKET SENTIMENT 

TRADE PLAN

LONG SHORT SPREAD

SYMBOL:

ENTRY PRICE:

TARGET PRICE:

STOP LOSS:

CLOSE PRICE:

STRATEGY:

SETUP CHART

ENTRY TIME: : AM/PM

CLOSE TIME: : AM/PM

PURCHASE PRICE:

CLOSING PRICE:

COMMISSION:

TRADE RESULT

PROFIT / LOSS: $

TRADE ANALYSIS

PERSONAL NOTES

TRADEJOURNAL

/ / M T W T F S S

MARKET
SENTIMENT

TRADE PLAN

LONG SHORT SPREAD

SYMBOL:

ENTRY PRICE:

TARGET PRICE:

STOP LOSS:

CLOSE PRICE:

STRATEGY:

SETUP CHART

ENTRY TIME: : AM/PM

CLOSE TIME: : AM/PM

PURCHASE PRICE:

CLOSING PRICE:

COMMISSION:

TRADE RESULT

PROFIT / LOSS: $

TRADE ANALYSIS

PERSONAL NOTES

/ / M T W T F S S

MARKET SENTIMENT

TRADE PLAN

LONG SHORT SPREAD

SYMBOL:

ENTRY PRICE:

TARGET PRICE:

STOP LOSS:

CLOSE PRICE:

STRATEGY:

SETUP CHART

ENTRY TIME: : AM/PM

CLOSE TIME: : AM/PM

PURCHASE PRICE:

CLOSING PRICE:

COMMISSION:

TRADE RESULT

PROFIT / LOSS: $

TRADE ANALYSIS

PERSONAL NOTES

TRADEJOURNAL

/ / M T W T F S S

MARKET SENTIMENT 

TRADE PLAN

LONG SHORT SPREAD

SYMBOL:

ENTRY PRICE:

TARGET PRICE:

STOP LOSS:

CLOSE PRICE:

STRATEGY:

SETUP CHART

ENTRY TIME: : AM/PM

CLOSE TIME: : AM/PM

PURCHASE PRICE:

CLOSING PRICE:

COMMISSION:

TRADE RESULT

PROFIT / LOSS: $

TRADE ANALYSIS

PERSONAL NOTES

MY NOTES

MY NOTES

MY NOTES

MY NOTES

NEED MORE INFO:

http://www.thetraderswire.com
info@thetraderswire.com

THE TRADER'S JOURNAL

www.thetraderswire.com

Made in the USA
Monee, IL
04 November 2026

67375604R00026